CONTENTS

Thirty Years' War

History for beginners

Circumstances, course and effects of
the Thirty Years' War and the long
road to peace

Markus Neustedt

What you can expect in this book

Dark clouds cast a shadow over 17th century Europe and color the continent in a dark fog. When they break out, a deluge of blood and sweat rolls over the countries, destroying landscapes and wiping out entire cities. There has never been a more merciless war in the history of Europe. Between state-building and religious conflicts, soldiers are sent to certain death and villages are razed to the ground. But how well do we know the circumstances under which Europe is carried into disaster? How are the people who are directly affected by the consequences of war faring?

The horror begins with a revolution that shakes the supremacy of the Habsburgs in Central Europe. More and more nations become entangled in the tangle of revenge and loyalty obligations. The newly emerged military enterprise made warfare a lucrative affair for princes and dukes. With the battles, the inhibitions against brutality and destructive mania faded. When the Catholic troops gather in front of the city walls of a Protestant stronghold, a devastating mass murder is in the offing. And when France and Spain declare war, the survival of the population is threatened.

But what happens to the people who don't go into battle? The poverty-stricken population has to face an unusual enemy: their own nation. Testimonies from days gone by tell of the terrible crimes committed against women in the villages. Farmers lose more than they own in the face of war and almost work themselves to death. The situation is particularly dangerous when diseases spread and the funeral pyres are used again.

The long road to peace is arduous and paved with cruelty. Almost half of the European population falls victim to the war. Impressions of their vices, the leading figures of the war and the most important battles await you in this book.

Europe's dark path

POVERTY, HUNGER & PESTILENCE

What image do you have of 17th century Europe? Imagine how a war could come about. You will no doubt remember that the great world wars did not break out overnight, but were based on various events and conflicts in previous years. The 17th century is no different. Europe's path to an apocalyptic war began long before the so-called "Defenestration of Prague" in 1618, traditionally understood as the outbreak of war.

Various crises plague the European population in the decades leading up to the catastrophe and drive the continent down a dark path. Economic emergencies, religious and state conflicts and disease harden the hearts and minds of all Europeans.

From as early as the 1560s, exceptional climatic conditions are recorded, which are referred to as a "little ice age". The coming winters are particularly harsh and protracted, the summers mostly wet and with low yields. These are disastrous conditions for a population that is dependent on the yields of local farmers, if not on their own crops. The quality of forests, stones and metals also suffers from the cold spell, making usable materials scarcer. The contemporary geographer Rüdiger Glaser also records a strikingly frequent occurrence of storms over Central Europe in 1612, and in 1615 even the wells begin to freeze over.

The situation is particularly difficult in the Holy Roman Empire of the German Nation, which has served as a land of immigration for over a century. Especially after the Religious Peace of Augsburg in 1555, the empire developed into a promising new home for Protestants in Europe. The population grew by almost 100% between 1500 and 1618, but as the number of citizens increased, the chance of finding a paid job decreased, at a time when merciless winters and poor summers led to rapidly rising food prices.

Alongside hunger, another deadly inhabitant roams the afflicted lands: it is the plague.

It is back and spreading via lice and fleas seeking warm shelter in the lush coats of freezing people. The Last Judgement is looming. At least that is how it seemed to the witnesses of the time, who interpreted the natural disasters in their Christian worldview as harbingers of the end times. And the idea is not that inaccurate.

STATE CONFLICTS

Europe witnesses a considerable list of wars that precede and pave the way for the Thirty Years' War. Their motives are different, but she will witness the disaster in which they all converge. In order to understand the causes of the horrors of the years to come, it is worth taking a broad overview of the major conflicts.

Emancipation of the Netherlands

"State-building war" is the keyword coined by historian Johannes Burkhardt in relation to the Thirty Years' War. In reality, this applies particularly to the Netherlands:

Based on an old legal conception, the Netherlands was regarded as part of the Holy Roman Empire in the 16th century. Nevertheless, Dutch attitudes increasingly distanced themselves from this affiliation. The first revolts against Habsburg rule broke out in 1566. The Habsburg King of Spain, Phillip II, currently exercised sovereignty over the important trading nation. The aim of the uprisings was to persuade the important provinces of Holland and Zeeland in particular to become independent. They are fighting for the freedom of their confessions and for more political autonomy - in opposition to the Catholic centralization sought by Phillip.

At the end of the 16th century, the northern provinces of the Netherlands asserted themselves against Spanish repression and formed a Calvinist alliance that sharply distinguished itself from the other provinces. This earned them the respect of the English crown and the Bourbons as allies.

However, the crisis became an increasing burden for the Kingdom of Spain. When Spain also intervened in the internal religious conflicts in France, the great power reached its limits. In 1596, the banks are empty.

The conflict seemed to be coming to an end when peace negotiations with the Netherlands began in 1607 under Phillip III. The Spanish regent expressed his acceptance of the Calvinist party's independence. However, this did not mean the end. The Dutch had little use for the Spanish peace terms. They were unwilling to guarantee either the toleration of Catholics or the cessation of their trade overseas. And so the conflict continued. At the end of July 1617, Phillip III signed the secret Oñate Treaty with the Habsburgs in Austria. He is prepared to sacrifice his succession to the throne in Bohemia and Hungary for the right to rule in Alsace, which opens up an important supply route for his troops in the Netherlands.

On this occasion of a possible new threat from Spain, the conflict between supporters and opponents of the peace course in the Netherlands came to a head. The important statesman Johann van Oldenbarnevelt argued for a cautious foreign policy, while Moritz von Oranienburg led the anti-Spanish movement. After the latter attends a church service of the radical peace resisters in the summer of 1617, an open conflict begins between the two parties. Johann van Oldenbarnevelt was beheaded in The Hague in 1619. The verdict: high treason. But the Spanish-Dutch war was only about to enter its second round.

Bastions of Christianity

Anyone who chooses the Netherlands as an ally has long been an enemy of the Habsburgs. The competition between France and Spain for European hegemony began 200 years earlier. Sovereignty over Italy and the west of the Holy Roman Empire of the German Nation was particularly coveted.

In 1601, the tide turns in favor of the French. France signs the Peace of Lyon with Savoy. As a result, the Spanish superpower loses an important supply route through Savoy. France also increasingly supported opponents of the Habsburgs in Europe. But Spain gets away with it for the time being. In 1610, the Bourbon King Henry IV was assassinated. In response, civil war breaks out in France. The conflict with Spain cooled for the time being, as Louis XIII had to worry about stabilizing his own state. However, the Thirty Years' War has not yet broken out.

The Goths against Denmark

More northern parts of Europe are also characterized by constant conflict. Since 1600, there have been military confrontations in the Baltic region. The protagonist is the rising superpower Sweden, which lays claim to the old empire by invoking its Gothic roots. Opposing them is the Kingdom of Denmark. The Danish King Christian IV ruled over Norway and the duchies of Schleswig and Holstein in addition to his homeland. He would not give up his Baltic region so quickly. After all, customs duties on the Sund Strait were one of the kingdom's main sources of income.

Sweden has become a worthy opponent in recent years. Especially under Gustav II Adolf's reform to promote Catholicism and centralization, the Swedish military grew in size and efficiency. However, Denmark was not the only thorn in the Swedish side. In 1617, they conquered Karelia and

Ingermanland against Russia and soon Poland was also at war with them.

"Long Turkish war"
The Ottoman Empire posed a new threat to Central Europe. Under Sultan Suleiman the Magnificent, the great power from the East has advanced to the borders of the Holy Roman Empire. Countries under Habsburg rule in particular, such as Hungary, had to prepare for a possible conflict.

In 1593, Sultan Murad III breaks the 25-year-old truce with the Emperor and begins the "long Turkish war" with a major campaign against Hungary, Bohemia and Austria. It was not until 1606 that the Sultan was forced to recognize the Emperor as an equal ruler and pay him a one-off tribute.

INNER DECAY

In the Holy Roman Empire itself, the conflict between the denominations grew and shook the solid Habsburg pillars. The fronts that form here will paint the destructive picture of the Thirty Years' War and contribute to merciless excesses of violence. The discord is based on a constitution that both parties are trying to turn in their favour and which is summarized below.

The imperial order and the search for compromise

It hardly resembles what you would understand by a proper constitution today. In the 17th century, the imperial order was made up of traditional conventions and isolated decisions from the past.

The Golden Bull: In 1356, the Golden Bull defined the Holy Roman Empire as an elective monarchy. Elections were held by the Electoral College, consisting of four secular and three ecclesiastical electors. The secular votes in the imperial election belong to the King of Bohemia, the Electors of Saxony, the Market Counts of Brandenburg and the Count Palatine. On the other side, the archbishops of Cologne, Mainz and Trier vote as spiritual representatives.

Land peace: Since 1495, the General Land Peace has prohibited the execution of vigilante justice through feuding. Failure to comply is punishable by breach of the peace and the loss of legal protection.

A reform of the imperial order in the middle of the 16th century gave the imperial estates more influence over the emperor. From now on, their voices were also heard when it came to tax approvals and new laws. In addition, the imperial estates were given jurisdiction. In 1600, the Imperial Chamber Court, which was virtually independent of the Emperor, was once again on solid ground. To ensure that imperial laws, judgments and the peace of the land were enforced, they set up imperial circles charged with executive power. At the same time, a separate court was constituted for the emperor, the Imperial Court of Justice, which ensured his function as a legal authority. The consequences of the imperial reform became problematic when several imperial estates converted to the Protestant faith, despite the prohibition in the Edict of Worms of 1521. This created legal complications for ecclesiastical princes before the imperial laws, because unlike the secular princes, the denomination of their territories was based on their own.

The resulting conflict seemed hopeless. Emperor Charles V's military attempts to bring the princes back to Catholicism also fail.

When Protestant uprisings were also successful in 1151/52, the Treaty of Passau was finally signed, promising peace between the religious factions. The efforts culminated in the Peace of Augsburg in 1555, which prohibited violence based on religious differences of opinion and even condemned it as a breach of the peace. This applies at least to the protection of Lutherans. Calvinists are still regarded as a sect and are not protected by law. Lutheran imperial estates may retain their denomination, but ecclesiastical princes may no longer change it.

The situation is coming to a head again
For a time, the Peace of Augsburg helped to preserve religious freedom and promote reasonably peaceful relations between the denominations. Now, however, it was the Catholics who felt disadvantaged and, from the 1570s onwards, increasingly wanted to assert themselves against the Protestants. Only with the support of several sovereigns could a Catholic reform and counter-reform be carried out, which strengthened the

Catholics' efforts to re-establish their denomination and spread it to Protestant followers.

The situation came to such a head that the Imperial Diet denied the Protestant administrator of Magdeburg the right to vote in 1582. Shortly afterwards, the Archbishop of Cologne was deposed by the Pope because he had broken his celibacy and converted to the Protestant faith. The archbishop leaves his Cologne to the Catholics - but not without resistance - and can only be driven away by force of arms.

After Protestants seize the flags of the Catholics during a Catholic procession through Donauwörth in 1607 and march through the filthy streets, the conflict in the empire reaches its zenith. The Archduke of Bavaria, Maximilian, sends his Catholic soldiers into the town and seizes it. The Protestants are condemned before the Imperial Court. Shortly after the capture, Maximilian begins to re-Catholicize the city. Archduke of Inner Austria and soon to be Holy Roman Emperor, Ferdinand of Styria, supported the Bavarian and in 1608 officially demanded that all Protestants return the Catholic church properties that had been "alienated" since 1552 to the care of the Catholics.

In response to this demand, the Lutheran Imperial Estates founded a union of Protestant supporters with their own army in May 1608. A year later, Maximilian of Bavaria responded with a newly founded Catholic League.

Defenestration of Prague

In historical tradition, the "Defenestration of Prague" marks the beginning of the Thirty Years' War. Above all, the role of Bohemia in European politics is decisive. Catholic Bohemia formed the majority in the Electoral College of the Holy Roman Empire. Their vote secured the role of Catholicism in the imperial election and thus also the Habsburgs' claim to be emperor.

The majority of the Bohemian population, including most of the nobility, had not been Catholics for some time, but believed in the teachings of the reformer Jan Hus. To the disillusionment of Bohemia, the pious Catholic and counter-reformer Ferdinand of Styria was elected to the Wenceslas crown under Emperor Matthias II in June 1617 and crowned in Prague. The following year, he also received the crown of Hungary.

The Protestant population watched their new king with increasing concern. Fear of a counter-reformation led to unrest in Bohemia. Emperor Matthias clumsily attempts to quell the unrest with a biting tone, but is met with an increasingly heated atmosphere.

On May 23, 1618, Protestant nobles in Prague's Hradcany Castle attempt to ask the Catholic governors to justify Emperor Matthias' reaction. Shortly afterwards, the discussion developed into a violent confrontation. Outraged, the nobles force two governors and their secretary into the Ludvik Wing. The Catholics are thrown out of the windows into the 17-metre-deep abyss - and survive.

But now the mood is one of revolution. The rebels set themselves up as a new parliament and elected a new government for Bohemia. One day later, their own army is formed and King Ferdinand II is forced to abdicate. The consequences are not long in coming and initiate the first major battle of the Thirty Years' War.

Battles of the damned

War is raging. And the first armies are getting ready to march towards the enemy camp. Battles after battles pile up on top of each other in no time at all. Which theaters shape the course of the war? Accompany the most important commanders on their campaigns through Europe and get an idea of the enormous scale of the war. A line of permanent conflict and devastation stretches from Prague across the Baltic Sea to southern Germany.

WINTER KING AND BLOOD COURT

1619-1625

There is a revolutionary mood in Prague. After the Defenestration of Prague and the expulsion of Ferdinand of Styria, Bohemia is faced with the question of a new guardian of the Wenceslas crown. A question whose answer would trigger the first great battle of the Thirty Years' War. After a pious Catholic king, it was now of great interest to the Bohemian government to finally be able to appoint a Protestant regent who would represent and support the confession of the majority. The new king must be a sign of the Prague government's autonomy and embody its claim to the Protestant denomination. News of Ferdinand's deposition soon reaches the Electoral Palatinate. The Protestant Elector Frederick V ruled here with his convinced Calvinist Chancellor Christian I of Anhalt-Bernburg. In his search for a new monarch, he recognizes the opportunity to weaken the Habsburgs' sphere of influence and thus also that of the Catholics. In order to win their favor, the chancellor sends military support to Prague. The

Prague government quickly offered the Elector Frederick the crown. His confession and good connections to the English royal family were particularly convincing of the Palatine nobleman's competence. Although his own council advised him against it, Frederick accepted the election as king in August 1619. In October, he arrives in Prague with his wife Elisabeth Stuart. A severe setback for the Habsburgs.

But things turn out differently than hoped. The new king quickly becomes unpopular with the people. His radical iconoclasm in particular caused his reputation to plummet. Revolts even began to form when Frederick V wanted to dismantle the icons on Charles Bridge in addition to St. Vitus Cathedral. Meanwhile, the Bohemian rebels try to expand their army in preparation for a possible revenge action with the Imperial Catholic League. Silesia joins the Prague rebels as early as October of the previous year. After the death of Matthias II, Emperor of the Holy Roman Empire of the German Nation, in March 1619, more German duchies dared to support Bohemia. They form the *Confoederatio Bohemica.* Matthias' successor is Ferdinand of Styria, now Ferdinand II. He immediately promises the leader of the Catholic League, Maximilian of Bavaria, the electoral dignity of the Palatinate if they are able to reconquer Bohemia and expel the new king. The first warring parties stand. The Confederation and the League soon clash.

After several successful campaigns towards Prague, the Imperial Catholic army led by general Johann von Tilly stands at the gates of the capital. A last desperate attempt to stop the advancing forces culminates in the Battle of White Mountain, which it is hoped will give the Bohemian troops a strategic advantage. But even the hill could not keep up with the strength of the League. On November 8, 1620, a brief skirmish took place. The Bohemian Confederation suffers its last and heaviest defeat to date. The Bohemian uprising collapses and Frederick, who stays in Hradcany Castle throughout the battle and tries to ask the English ambassadors for support, flees into exile in the Netherlands.

After the reconquest of Bohemia, Ferdinand II shows little consideration. The emperor wanted to set an example. He imposes 27 death sentences, some of them arbitrary. Ten Bohemian noblemen and 17 peasants are on the blacklist. The victims were usually only informed of their sentence a few days beforehand. On June 21, 1621, the Emperor had a stage erected in front of the Old Town Hall. The beheading and hanging continued for four hours, with several blades being worn down. To add to the humiliation, the drummers played so loudly that the last words of the condemned could not be heard. The bloody act of revenge achieves its effect. To warn of future uprisings, the Emperor also has 12 of the severed heads attached to the bridge tower leading to the Old Town, where they will be mounted on long lances for 10 years, bearing witness to the horrors of the "Prague Blood Tribunal" and the first great battle of the Thirty Years' War. The Bohemian lands are mainly sold to Catholic nobles in the empire.

Frederick's homeland also fared badly. In 1622, Maximilian I of Bavaria seized what the emperor had promised him. The capital Heidelberg is set on fire, soldiers plunder silver and gold and the Biblioteca Palatina, one of the most important repositories of medieval literature, is completely transferred to the Vatican. Catholicism is imposed on the Electoral Palatinate and all Protestant clergy are expelled by 1625.

No glorious testimony to the Protestant Union remains of Frederick V's brief reign in Bohemia. Only the degrading title "Winter King" tells of the fatal reign under Frederick, which lasted a short time and did anything but weaken the power of the Habsburgs.

Tip:

Visit the Old Town Hall in Prague today. There you will find 27 white crosses embedded in the floor. You can get an impression of the culture of remembrance in Bohemia.

DENMARK AND WALLENSTEIN

1624-1628/29

After the Bohemian uprisings are crushed, two leaders of the former Winter King's mercenary troops flee to Lower Saxony. Christian von Braunschweig and Ernst von Mansfeld use the region to provide for their soldiers. The soldiers consumed supplies and much of the labor of the local farmers. But they impose a further burden on the towns of Lower Saxony. Through their presence, the Protestant commanders may provoke a violent re-Catholicization by the League, whose troops are stationed not far away. To prevent this, the estates of Lower Saxony devised a plan to distract the imperial troops with the threat of a European war. Lower Saxony seeks support from Christian IV of Denmark in particular. The Danish king had sovereignty over Holstein and was also a member of the Lower Saxon circle.

The Nordic kingdom conquers several cities in northern Germany shortly beforehand. Soon the Danish crown is also enthroned over the particularly influential city of Hamburg. Strengthened, Christian now declares himself under the protection of Lower Saxony, but is slow to act. Christian of Brunswick first attempts to bring events under his control in the spring of 1623, but the Catholic League responds to his armament efforts to reconquer Bohemia by advancing as far south as Lower Saxony. At the Battle of Stadtlohn, the experienced Johann von Tilly brought Brunswick's efforts to a standstill.

Christian IV initially remains cautious. He was concerned that Sweden might conquer parts of the Baltic Sea and Denmark during his engagement with Lower Saxony. The monarch also hoped for reinforcements from France and England.

The turning point came in 1624. James I, King of England, no longer negotiated peace with the Spanish Habsburgs and went on the offensive. At the same time, France, which had been hostile to the Emperor for some time, also tightened its fronts against the Emperor under the foreign policy of Cardinal Richelieu. Towards the end of the year, the States General declare their official alliance with Denmark. The following year, a new army from Lower Saxony is formed under the leadership of Christian IV. The Emperor issued a mandate in an attempt to prevent Lower Saxony from rearming. In order to ensure its implementation, Tilly's imperial troops march into Lower Saxony's war zone.

The time is ripe for another protagonist in the Thirty Years' War. The Viennese royal court discusses an offer they can hardly refuse. In 1625, the noble Duke Albrecht von Wallenstein, who also owns territory in Bohemia, offers the Emperor to raise his own army to support the imperial troops in view of the tensions on the border with Lower

Saxony. In the late fall of that year, the military entrepreneur brings a full 40,000 mercenaries under his command, with whom he joins Tilly. In the months that followed, the tide turned dramatically in the Emperor's favor. The Huguenots rebel in France and the English king starts a war with Spain. Their support for Denmark wanes.

Christian IV underestimates the situation. When the imperial troops were distracted by peasant uprisings in 1626, the Danish monarch felt ready to fight. The Danish army is defeated at Lutter am Barenberg and the Lower Saxon alliance collapses. During the winter, many of the county estates are forced to reaffirm their loyalty to the Emperor. The hero against the Danes, Wallenstein, who had provided the Emperor with a huge army and led it himself, marched further north. The general captures Schleswig, Holstein and Jutland, finally driving the Danes from German soil. Christian IV orders the retreat.

PARTISAN FRONT

1626-1630s

Wallenstein's army comes at just the right time for the emperor. However, the population largely despised the soldiers. In 1625, the Harz region in particular was burdened by the presence of the Catholic soldiers and terrorized by them. The following year, the farmers and craftsmen formed an armed alliance. Dressed as hunters, the 600 to 800 men call themselves the "Freye Harzschützen". Their knowledge of the region gave them the bitterly needed advantage to cause unrest among the imperial army. They transformed the Harz region into an unsafe country for the soldiers. In July 1627, they managed to storm Klettenberg Castle and Stiege. In doing so, however, they arouse the full vengeful wrath of the League.

Shortly afterwards, the imperial soldiers capture the stronghold of Beckenstein and other refuges of the Freyen Harzschützen. It is not long before the importance of the partisans disappears.

Only once, after the destruction of Magdeburg in 1631, do they reappear for a short time.

Their chapter may have been short and insignificant for the course of the Thirty Years' War, but their story shows that war is actually always waged over the heads of the population. It is not a patriotic test of loyalty, but a degradation of civilian interests. The Freyen Harzschützen tried in vain to defend themselves against this tyranny by the emperor.

Tip:
Compare the Freyen Harzschützen with other peasant or civil uprisings during the Thirty Years' War. What do you think were important factors for a successful resistance?

THE LION OF SWEDEN

1630-1634

In 1630, the Emperor faced the greatest threat of the Thirty Years' War. Never before had his sovereignty been so threatened. Sweden decides to join the European conflict - ostensibly under the pretext of supporting the endangered and subjugated Protestants in Germany.

The Swedes can refer to an old legacy of the Gothic Empire. It is the claim to rule the majority of the world. And this claim was jeopardized by the expansion of the Habsburgs.

Imperial Catholic troops occupy Wismar in 1627. The city on the Baltic coast is soon declared a port of war for the Emperor. A disaster for the great power Sweden, which wanted to take control of the Baltic region. Their plans were expressly thwarted in 1628 when Rostock fell into the hands of the Catholics and an imperial naval fleet was built. The Habsburgs' famous war hero, Wallenstein, was even appointed "General of the Baltic and Oceanic Seas".

Gustav Adolf, King of Sweden, decides to counteract this expansion. He knows Germany from a secret journey in 1620 and knows how to make appropriate preparations.

In May 1630, the king crossed the Baltic Sea with 13,000 soldiers. Two months later, he sets foot on Usedom. The imperial troops there immediately flee at the sight of the great power. A miracle comes true for the Protestants in Germany. After the defeat of Denmark, they see the Swedish king as the savior of their denomination. To underline his glory, Gustav Adolf is called the "Lion of Midnight", whose myth-like appearance awakens hope in Protestant hearts.

And the Swedish campaign proves to be an enormous success early on. After forming an alliance with Pomerania on July 20, the Swedish army occupies Anklam and Wolgast. Exactly two months later, Stralsund and the Duchy of Mecklenburg, previously owned by Wallenstein, belong to the Swedish kingdom.

Gustav Adolf moves further south with his army. In April 1631, he conquers Landsberg an der Warthe and Frankfurt an der Oder.

Then it becomes urgent. The Swedes try to reach Magdeburg in a quick march to save the Protestant trading town threatened by the imperial commanders Tilly and Pappenheim from destruction. The rescue comes too late. Although the Swedes capture nearby Berlin and Potsdam, they are unable to prevent the horror. Magdeburg falls under the cruelest conditions. Although the Protestant stronghold is lost, it awakens the spirit of resistance of Protestants throughout the empire. Gustav Adolf is now clearly seen as a savior figure against the Catholic supremacy, which was still so despised. Pamphlets tell of Gustav's victories and incite the Protestants against the Austrian tyranny.

Meanwhile, the Swedes continue to advance. In July, they occupied Havelberg and defeated Tilly's army at Breitenfeld. The advantage of the Swedes is the rapid rate of fire of their guns and their sophisticated formations, which allow greater mobility. Wernigerode and Erfurt fall in September, the Thuringian Forest and Schweinfurt in October. Frankfurt am Main and Mainz fall into Swedish hands in December. Gustav Adolf has reached the climax of his reign. A large region of central Germany, from north to south, is conquered by his army in a very short time. Wismar, Rostock and Dömitz are added to the list. The emperor's naval career comes to a standstill and his power is mercilessly diminished. His own people turn against him. Only a tenth of the 150,000 or so under Gustav Adolf are Scandinavians. Alongside Scots and Italians, German Protestants in particular join the fight against the emperor.

In March 1632, the whole of Nuremberg celebrates the arrival of the Swedes. They seem untouchable. But one fear plagues the heirs of the

Gothic Empire - the scarce financial remains bear witness to the large-scale campaign.

To finance his army, Gustav Adolf has high levies collected from the newly fallen Augsburg in April. Perhaps it was an attempt at appeasement that prompted the king to attend a Catholic church service, but the levies from his newly subjugated territories also came too late. Blinded by victory, he pushes his financial strength to the limit. The severe shortfalls become apparent when he lacks the means to take Ingolstadt in April. Defeated, the king withdraws his army. But that is not enough.

In Swabia and Bavaria, the peasants begin to resist the troublesome soldiers and mercenaries. The Swedes are forced to entrench themselves in Nuremberg when news spreads that Wallenstein has announced his intention to support the rebels. Gustav Adolf succeeds in defending the city against Wallenstein's mercenary forces until the end of August, but hunger and disease plague the Swedes. There are no more supplies from which to take food or medicine, so Gustav takes on the decisive battle against the Imperial forces.

On November 16, 1632, the two armies meet at Lützen. It actually appears that Sweden wins the battle, but around midday the battlefield is covered by a thick fog.

Unconsciously, Gustav Adolf rides into the midst of the enemy soldiers that the fog has hidden from him. After several shots, the beloved king falls from his horse and dies from his bullet wounds.

The Swedes win the battle, but with the fall of the lion, so too does the thirst for action. His body is brought to the church in Wittenberg. A symbolic place. Luther posted his theses on its doors. The king, who died fighting for the Protestants, spends a night in the birthplace of the Reformation. And Wallenstein? It is the perfect moment to strike and perhaps even drive the Swedes from German soil, but the experienced commander does not react. For the entire year of 1633, he put all military efforts against the Swedes on hold. When he renounces the liberation of Regensburg, which had been subjugated by the Swedes, in 1634, skepticism spreads at the Viennese court. It was the beginning of a tragedy.

Emperor Ferdinand II is told of intrigues. Wallenstein himself was interested in the imperial crown. He even allied himself with the Swedes. Perhaps the truth? Or evil-minded voices? Ferdinand II takes action. He orders the assassination of Wallenstein. On February 24, 1634, the general receives his reward for his loyal service since 1625. He is stabbed to death by the Irishman Walter Deveroux.

In the summer of 1634, the Catholic League expels Sweden from southern Germany after the Battle of Nördlingen.

MAGDEBURG BLOOD WEDDING

A city in flames. No event in the Thirty Years' War makes history like the destruction of Magdeburg. The attack is almost representative of the war and is regarded as the darkest testimony to its violent madness. For contemporaries, it is particularly terrible. Traumas and fears spread. Magdeburg becomes a spectre, a symbol of the omnipresent decay and the insecurity of violent attacks. Even the word "magdeburgizing" becomes commonplace and describes total destruction.

It is May 20, 1631. 22,000 of Tilly's imperial soldiers gather in front of the city walls. They are joined by around 6,000 mercenaries under the leadership of his deputy Pappenheim. The city in front of them is one of the largest and richest cities of the time. Its strategic location and fertile cornfields made it a coveted object. The problem: early on, the people of Magdeburg decided in favor of Martin Luther's teachings. Catholics were clearly in the minority. Nevertheless, the city tried to maintain its neutrality during the war. Now the plan seems to be crumbling. Despite the impending danger from Johann von Tilly, the people of Magdeburg decide against the offer of surrender. They hope for support from the Swedish army.

Around 7 a.m., the time has come: Johann von Tilly wants to take the city by force. A heavy bombardment hits Magdeburg first. The soldiers, especially the Pappenheimers, then enter the city. They are the ones who quickly start to light fires, which have a venerating effect during the course of the "conquest". The sudden defencelessness of the inhabitants of Magdeburg prompted the Pappenheim soldiers to take a particularly violent stance. They are no longer masters of their senses and spread unimagined horror in the city. The most horrific crimes suffered by the people of Magdeburg in this terrible hour of European history were the impaling of babies and the endless rape of girls and women. The brutality of the soldiers was said to be so merciless that even Tilly and Pappenheim were shocked and incomprehensible. It was not their intention to destroy the strategically favorable town. Their intention was to capture it for their own purposes. But the soldiers overrode them and razed the city to the ground. Even the right of asylum in the churches was abolished. Only the few who took refuge in Magdeburg Cathedral were spared by the soldiers. In the end, most of the buildings have disappeared, giving way to epidemics and the smell of decay. Of the original 35,000 inhabitants, around 450 remain in the end.

Tip:

Take a look (also on the Internet) at illustrations of the Magdeburg Wedding. From these you can see what impression such an extermination campaign made on contemporaries.

L'ART DE LA GUERRE

1634-1638

After the Swedes are driven back, the European battlefield expands. The French feel compelled to officially join the Great War. Cardinal Richelieu's intention as a foreign politician is to strengthen the Swedes' backing in the remaining Baltic region in order to present himself as an attractive, if not necessary, ally.

This is of great importance to France because the kingdom has been heading for war with the feared Spain for some time. The two superpowers have been making preparations for a military conflict since 1632. The Spanish Road was at the center of this. A supply route leading from Italy to the Netherlands. For France, the conquest of the supply route by Spain would pose a threat and also mean the conquest of French sovereignty. For this reason, both parties increasingly stationed themselves along the Rhine. This only served to fuel a possible outbreak of conflict.

Sweden and the Netherlands have been on the side of the French since 1634. They were worried about the growing power of the Habsburgs and therefore entered into an alliance with the Bourbons. Spain, on the other hand, enforced an alliance with the Emperor by ceasing to pay its taxes to Vienna. The loss of the Habsburgs' fundamental source of money risked a loss of power for the emperor and a halt to his reconquest of the empire. In October, the Viennese government accepts the Spanish Habsburgs' claim to military support from the imperial Catholic troops.

The escalation occurred when Spain occupied Trier in March 1635 without any foreseeable basis and captured the Elector. This forced France to act. The kingdom, which was actually still looking for alliances, had to stop recruiting and make a decision. On May 19, 1635, Louis XIII declared the capture of the Elector to be a breach of international law, thus justifying the official declaration of war on Spain. The conflict that broke out between France and Spain added far-reaching territories in Europe to the effects of the Thirty Years' War and extended the focus from the Holy Roman Empire to the whole of Europe. For 25 years, i.e. beyond the Thirty Years' War, the feud between France and Spain endures. The situation is so exhausting that the nations slowly begin to replace the endless killing, starvation and sickness with a desire for peace. But the road to a truce is difficult and takes a long time.

Testimonies of horror

From today's perspective, it will probably be impossible to capture the full, terrifying atmosphere of the battlefield during the Thirty Years' War. What remains for us are individual, scattered testimonies of that time, in which people's everyday realities were characterized by fear and suffering. What worries plagued the common people and what vices did the soldiers struggle with? What role did women play in the war? What do you know about the many merciless witch trials that flared up again amidst all the destruction?

THE LIFE OF THE MERCENARIES - PETER HAGENDORF

If the words "army" and "soldiers" make you think of strong men who fearlessly go from battle to battle, the fragments about soldiering in the Thirty Years' War will present you with a different world. The soldiers were by no means strong. Reports bear witness to men plagued by hunger and epidemics, their thin and tattered rags covering their emaciated bones. Life in the military is not only hard, it is also short. A Swedish study has shown that the average mercenary survives three years and four months of war. With more than thirty years, this is a sobering realization. But how can you imagine the unfortunate ones who are condemned to a difficult fate?

With the rise of the "military enterprise", the importance of mercenaries grows. They come from all over the world, including Scotland, Ireland and Italy, to join the war effort in return for a secure salary. They often wear colorful clothing enhanced with feathers or adorned with decorations. This distances them from civil society, to which they usually do not feel they belong. If they do not bring their own equipment, they have to pay a lot of money to buy it themselves. The muzzle-loader is a particularly popular weapon of choice. The diary of a mercenary who fought for the Catholic army in the Holy Roman Empire has been preserved. His notes summarize his life and give us an insight into the career of the foot soldier.

Peter Hagendorf is the name associated with the diary that has survived to this day. In 1627, he joins the Catholic army for 4 thalers a month. He immediately writes about what moves him. In 1631, he witnesses the destruction of Magdeburg. His contribution was small, and he was seriously wounded by two shots right at the beginning of the conquest. Peter can count himself lucky, as he not only survives his injuries, but also gains a job as a list clerk in a military hospital thanks to his ability to read and write. This spares him the coming battles for the time being. Nevertheless, the Thirty Years' War takes a hard and sad toll on him. The mercenary, who walked some 22,500 km during his service and witnessed various atrocities, lost seven of his nine children in the final years of assassination and murder.

WITH THE ENTOURAGE

The idea that only men take part in battles and plunder the land left behind is outdated. A colorful bunch of civilians are always there when the sword is drawn. This includes a large number of women. The so-called "Tross" is extremely versatile and takes care of the soldiers' supplies. It always moves with the army and can even be 3 to 4 times its size. Various professional groups are brought together in the Tross. Logisticians, doctors and craftsmen, but also sutlers and brewers are responsible for the needs of the troops. In the Middle Ages, sutlers took care of the soldiers' personal effects. Field smiths try to maintain the quality of the weapons, while brewers produce useful meals. Barbers take care of the hygienic needs and preachers satisfy the urge for spiritual presence. Soothsayers and esotericists mingle with the people, as do refugees and prostitutes. Of course, the cavalcade is also constantly accompanied by numerous farm animals.

The so-called "soldiers' wives" are particularly interesting. These women do not wait at home for their husbands to return, but go with them along with their families. They take care of the tent, the most necessary household chores and the children they bring with them. Occasionally, the women also took part in the looting and plundered the corpses on the battlefields.

WOMEN AT WAR - ELISABETH GEMMEROTH AND THE DIS-COVERY OF INHUMANITY

Elisabeth Gemmeroth lives in a troop. The officer's wife fulfills all the duties that she takes for granted as a wife of the time. And if it weren't for the battles and epidemics, she might have the impression that she was leading a completely normal life. But the army marches and the retinue follows. From Rostock via Italy back to Stendal, the never-ending line of people runs, bringing battle after battle behind them. As with most people robbed by war, not much is known about Elisabeth Gemmeroth's life. Only the graves of her children, found in 4 different places, testify to their existence; only one son survives. And Elisabeth? She dies in battle. As the battle between the Empire and the Swedes rages near Wittstock, the soldier's wife tries to flee. Not knowing the way, she is caught in the middle of the turmoil and suffers a fatal wound. Her heart stopped beating on October 4, 1636. A sermon written on the occasion of her funeral tells her story.

But what happens to the women who stayed at home? Imagine you are a woman in the Thirty Years' War. You are probably wondering what effects the war has on you. In short, you are on your own. It is women who have to experience what are probably the worst of all crimes against humanity. Monastery brothers in particular provide impressions of the horror that the violent soldiers spread throughout the villages and towns. They tell of mass rapes, a not inconsiderable number of which lead to the death of innocent women. Those who have not been violated to their last breath are mutilated, drowned or left to their trauma. Women who are lucky enough to be spared the brutal attacks have to watch all their possessions disappear into thin air. Whenever soldiers remain in a region, they consume an unsustainable amount of supplies, which they take by force from the surrounding villages and towns if necessary.

There are villages that are plundered around 18 times.

A NATION BURNS

Witchcraft! You have been accused. Plundering soldiers, hunger and deadly plagues make your life a burden, and now you are also accused of witchcraft. As incomprehensible as your accuser's reasoning may seem to you, there is little chance of salvation.

The situation is particularly fatal for women in the Holy Roman Empire of the German Nation. Never before have so many burnt-out pyres dominated the silhouettes of German villages. The most witches in the world were executed here. The increased search for scapegoats is certainly linked to the crop failures, pandemics and the horrors of war, as the cold-blooded trials following the Reformation had largely subsided by the 1520s. The persecution of witches was not a state commandment. The autonomous administration of most regions allowed for uncontrollable vigilante justice. The population was guided by the prominent "Hexenhammer" ("Hammer of Witches") by the clergyman Heinrich Kramer. In it, he spreads his ideas about the symptoms of witchcraft, how to deal with a witch and what course a witch trial should take. The work does not help them. It is highly unlikely that they can read, or Latin for that matter. And so they have few options to protect themselves from arbitrary persecution. If you follow Kramer's instructions, you can imagine a typical witch trial in this way. First, a person has to be accused of being a supposed witch or sorcerer. Personal disputes often play a major role in this. The accused person then ends up in prison and has to wait in cold dungeons or cells for further proceedings. This is followed by interrogation, usually in three phases, in which torture is usually used. A witch trial is also possible, which is intended to uncover the demonic alliance with the devil. Either way, the victims are usually forced to confess. Before the witch is burned, she is usually asked whether she knows about other witches. An opportunity to take revenge on people or to hope in vain for a reduction in the punishment.

During the Thirty Years' War, around 25,000 innocent people fall victim to the excesses of the witch craze. Bamberg and Würzburg are among the strongholds. In addition to women, a few men also die. Their names are usually blown away by the wind along with their ashes.

However, science journalist Eva-Maria Schnurr writes about one name. Even if it is rare, a witch trial does not always end fatally. The name is Christine Meurer. She is the landlady of the Swan Inn. She is accused of witchcraft and sorcery by 19 citizens of the small town of Büdingen. The executioner uses several methods of torture to extract a confession from Christine. But Christine remains strong and this makes her a special case in the story. Despite being hung from a pulley, which dislocates her shoulder joints, and despite the thumbscrew that splinters her bones, Christine refuses to give in. She does not accept the accusation that she is a witch. In fact, the court gives up. Christine is allowed or forced to leave the country. The only condition: Christine must never talk about the trial. The officials fear an act of revenge by the woman, whom they still believe to be a witch.

How do you feel about literature? Do you find it difficult to read poetry, or are you moved by the blunt statements? Poems and songs are an important testimony to past worlds. They actually always report on the thoughts that move a society or an individual.

Journalist Michael Sontheimer has written about a poet during the Thirty Years' War. It is the Protestant pastor Paul Gerhardt. The soon-to-be poet was born in March 1607, so he was only eleven years old when the Catholic governors were thrown out of the window of Hradcany Castle and war gradually broke out in Europe. Disaster thus accompanies him for the majority of his life. His life was marked by loss from an early age. His parents died while he was still young and his siblings died a little later from the plague. The single man studied theology for 15 years before moving to Berlin in 1643, where he wrote his Christian songs. He wrote poetry about faith and hope. His songs convey hope through their light-heartedness. In particular, the pastor tries to help his wife with her depression after the death of their son.

However, Paul's songs quickly found more listeners. His 139 songs have been handed down in Protestant and Catholic songbooks. Hope has always been the most important asset for surviving a crisis. Hope is the only thing that Pandora leaves to mankind after bringing all kinds of misery upon them. It is embodied in Paul Gerhardt's songs. He writes poetry:

"How you and others often fare
Is truly not hidden from him;
He sees and knows from on high
The sorrows of afflicted hearts.
He counts the course of the hot tears And comprehends
all our longings."

> **Tip**:
> Literature: Read the "adventurous Simplicissimus". The contemporary novel gives further impressions of life and feelings during the Thirty Years' War

A new world

Years and years pass, villages are uprooted and entire towns disappear under the devastating violence of the Thirty Years' War. The plague of brutality and epidemics seemed never to want to leave the European countries. But as great as the thirst for war and the stubbornness of the parties may be, the many hardships eventually drive the continent to war-weariness. Nevertheless, you must not imagine peace as a tangible goal. Several years of tedious negotiations, accompanied by further battles, stand in the way of a final peace.

The first hope for an end to the suffering is kindled on German soil of all places, which is scarred like no other by the violent destruction of war. Presumably for this very reason, the first step towards a European ceasefire is taken here. No population is as exhausted as the Germans. The Holy Roman Empire of the German Nation is not only the scene of its own conflicts, but also, since the latest developments, of conflicts between Sweden, France and Spain.

To mark the beginning of a universal peace, Emperor Ferdinand II and Elector of Saxony John George conclude a peace treaty in Prague. Saxony had previously been an ally of Sweden. After the death of its king, the electorate distanced itself from the Swedes. Johann Georg wanted to teach the stubborn emperor a military lesson, but the elector was averse to a foreign ruler in the empire. The death of Gustav Adolf, with whom he had personally entered into the alliance, served Johann Georg as a reason to dissolve it. For this reason, the Emperor and the Elector come closer together, leading to the signing of the peace treaty in Prague on May 30, 1635. The astonishing thing about the Peace of Prague is its innovative circumstances for the time, because although the peace was actually only made between two people, the important document applied to the entire empire.

The Protestant imperial estates are urgently recommended to recognize the peace. Enough of them do so. For the first time in several decades, the conflicts between the parties in the empire come to rest. Imperial peace is considered to have been restored. The news is distributed in all directions via print media and explains the legitimacy of the peace to the imperial estates and princes. There are concessions on both the Catholic and Protestant sides. All special alliances are dissolved and the armed forces of the empire once again gather behind the emperor to form a large imperial army.

But that was not enough. The Saxon Elector Johann Georg in particular tries to convince the Swedes of the Peace of Prague, as they are also offered the truce. However, the situation has changed. Due to their recent commitment to anti-Habsburg France, the Swedes refrain from joining the Peace of Prague. The Universal Peace thus collapses. A new era of war unfolds as a result of the tensions between France and Spain, which are to surpass the previous extent of the war. Germany in particular suffers from its merciless use as a theater of war.

BETWEEN MURDER AND DINING

The war continues for another five years before the prospect of a European peace emerges. The new period of war drives Germany in particular to exhaustion. The imperial estates and princes of the Empire expressly call on the Emperor to join the forthcoming peace negotiations. With the new imperial army, it occurred to Emperor Ferdinand III that a victory for the Holy Roman Empire was still possible. Not so the nobles under his crown. They persistently persuaded the Emperor to sign the Preliminary Peace of Hamburg in 1641, opening the doors to a new chapter in Europe that was sorely needed. Without the Emperor's concessions to make peace, the survival of the entire German nation, which had already lost half of its population, was threatened.

In 1644, peace negotiations begin in Osnabrück and Münster after all the representatives of the warring parties have finally arrived. These included Emperor Ferdinand III, the princes and imperial estates, Sweden, France and even the Netherlands and Spain.

In Osnabrück, the Emperor negotiates mainly with the Swedes and the Evangelists, who are still allies, while he meets France in Münster. When peace was negotiated, war was still raging. Sweden, France and Spain in particular try to make gains through simultaneous battles that support their demands and positions in the negotiations. Soldiers continue to die on the battlefields and the citizens continue to face the burden of plundering and decay-induced plagues, while the representatives of their nations in discussion move into luxurious quarters and dine on gold dishes. The negotiations are so lavish that almost all nations fall into deep debt. It is not surprising that corruption is not neglected at the meeting. Certain demands can only be accepted with an appropriate dowry.

The Imperial Estates expect the Emperor to dissolve the alliance with Spain in order to appease France. In fact, peace was already established with Sweden in 1645, as it would otherwise have occupied the important imperial city of Dresden. Spain grants the Dutch provinces their independence in January 1648. Of particular importance are the resolutions that all denominations in the Empire will be considered equal in the future. The imperial statesman Maximilian von und zu Trauttmansdorff, who demonstrated a talent for reconciling and mediating between nations, was extremely helpful in drafting the treaty. Only with Spain did he encounter hardened fronts.

Nevertheless, after several years of peace negotiations, in which the still exorbitant warfare should not be underestimated, the Peace of Westphalia was signed on October 24, 1648, officially ending the Thirty Years' War. The last blood-soaked battle in Bohemia only ended nine days after the agreement. The European population almost perished in its most terrible catastrophe to date.

Although the news of the peace agreement spreads general joy, there is still fear of a possible further outbreak of war. The war may have officially ended, but all the mercenaries still remained in the country. And while the population speaks enthusiastically of peace, France is less euphoric. However, the Bourbons are also preoccupied with the civil war.

But why is it that people have been fighting each other for 30 years despite being tired of war? After all, German citizens have been pleading for peace since the beginning of the war. And even successful military leaders like Wallenstein soon showed themselves to be peaceful. A fundamental problem of past wars is the concept of "honorable peace". Unlike today's understanding, this is not about an immediate ceasefire, but about negotiating one's own political interests. A militarily viable situation was usually of the greatest importance. Peace could prevail, so to speak, if the nation was theoretically capable of another outbreak of war. The fact that each nation had its own ideas of a militarily just starting position meant that agreement on peace was delayed. It was not until 1645, for example, that the emperor, whose population suffered the most deaths, was persuaded by Dresden and Vienna to lower his own demands and take the needs of the other nations into consideration.

Today, historians differ in their assessment of the Peace of Westphalia. What everyone considers progressive is the idea that there can be no overlord over Europe. The system of multiple states as we know it today is accepted. However, there is also criticism of the fact that it did not lead to the eternal peace that was sought. Spain and France continued to fight and the nations were not particularly tolerant in the years to come. Nevertheless, we find the diplomatic assembly as a recurring and formative element of future peace negotiations, such as at the Congress of Vienna at the beginning of the 19th century.

What remains

The war of annihilation devastates Europe for three decades, leaving behind nothing but pale memories of reasonably peaceful and familiar realities of life. What remains for a population that has witnessed the darkest hour of its existence? The consequences of the war have a devastating effect on the generations of that time and those to come.

CONSEQUENCES

Nothing establishes itself more explicitly in war than the omnipresence of death. Even before the

Thirty Years' War, life in the Middle Ages was to be enjoyed with caution. In other words, death is nothing new. Although wounds could already be healed well in the 16th century, if the illness had a cause that doctors could not immediately see, they usually relied on religious methods of treatment. It is therefore not surprising that there is a high mortality rate among people suffering from "invisible" diseases. Compared to the effects of the Thirty Years' War, however, this number seems negligible. Of the entire population of Europe, especially Central Europe, around 40% fell victim to the consequences of the war. There are even areas where up to 70 % of the original population died.

The result is a collective trauma that lasts for several generations in some areas, such as Magdeburg. The devastation left behind is particularly evident in Bohemia. An estimated 1000 villages were burned to the ground here. Around 250 castles and a whole 100 towns were also destroyed. The people are scarred by the horrors they witness. An English report from 1636 lists the following atrocities committed by soldiers: In addition to rape and witch-burning, crushing the skull, hanging people over a fire, working on the face with a chisel and hammer and the Swedish drink also appear. A mixture of slurry and excrement is poured into the victim's mouth, causing terrible burns in the stomach and often resulting in death.

Torn-down houses, fields eradicated to the point of barrenness and worn-out supplies contribute to the crisis during and after the war. Hunger remains one of the greatest plagues. In addition to the ongoing ice age, the broken fields prevent the cultivation of basic foodstuffs. Sources even report cannibalism in particularly affected areas.

While France and Great Britain got off rather lightly, developments in Germany were sluggish. Unlike the larger states, the Reich takes a century to recover. It is not until around 1700 that the population rises again. But there were also places in the Empire that benefited from the war. Hamburg and Bremen, for example, along with Strasbourg, Switzerland and the Netherlands, were among the places of refuge for German refugees. All of Europe's trade routes are increasingly focused on the West, where a better life is possible.

The war also had consequences for the estates of the Holy Roman Empire. The nobility in particular felt threatened. The nobility lost power and authority due to the increased loss of sovereignty and the difficulty of protecting their own estates during the war. Protestant nobles in particular found it increasingly difficult to provide for their families. The sense of justice fostered by the Peace of Westphalia also meant that the nobles were obliged to do more bureaucracy than before. If the subjects commit injustice against the lord of the manor, the matter must first go to trial and cannot be handled with blind threats or sanctions as before. The nobles were also concerned about the peasants' new self-confidence, which was linked to their being armed in war. The nobles were increasingly forced to join the service of the princes. This made them more dependent and at the same time strengthened the importance of the princely estate. This was a particularly profitable investment for the Viennese imperial court. It granted territories - mostly from the East, especially Bohemia - to nobles, thus creating a strong economic alliance. The Viennese imperial court was also one of the few to emerge from the war with a profit.

Life in the countryside is even more depressing. Although arming the peasants helps them to become more independent and makes it easier to buy a farm for a short time, rural life remains un-profitable and thankless. This is mainly due to the lack of usable land. This is why they flee to cities, where they hope to find a reasonably decent basic income. One problem is the severe epidemics that spread mainly in the alleyways of the streets and have a harder time in the countryside. This does not make the decision to flee the countryside for the city easy.

Overpopulation often occurs in cities thanks to the large numbers of refugees. This destroys the established economic systems by creating a sur-plus of labor, whereby the supply of the many new citizens is not guaranteed.

SPIRIT OF DISASTER

The Thirty Years' War remains anchored in pe-ople's consciousness for a long time and disturbs them with terrible memories or fears of renewed outbreaks of conflict. *Memento mori* and *vanitas* became the main pillars of Baroque art and poetry and bear witness to the terrifying impressions of the Thirty Years' War. Friedrich Schiller also wrote about the catastrophe and even wrote a play about Wallenstein. The war continued its horror in the spirit of the nation. The historian Johannes Burkhardt calls it the "war of wars". The poet Andreas Gryphius packs the full extent of its cruelty into the awe-inspiring verses of his "Tears of the Fatherland":

"Has all sweat and diligence
and stock has been spent.
The towers are ablaze,
the church is turned upside down.
The town hall lies in the gray,
the coffins are in ruins.
The maidens are defiled
and wherever we look there
is fire, plague and death" ~ *around 1636/37*

Tip:

Baroque poems often bear witness to the memory of death. *Memento mori* means something like "be aware of your mortality". *Vanitas* should serve as a constant reminder of earthly decay.

Read through baroque poems. You will certainly often encounter the constant presence of a sombre undertone. They are a piece of memory culture

---